The Olympic Spirit

Nicolas Brasch

The Olympic Spirit

Text: Nicolas Brasch
Publishers: Tania Mazzeo and Eliza Webb
Series consultant: Amanda Sutera
Hands on Heads Consulting
Editor: Jess Mackay
Project editor: Annabel Smith
Designer: Leigh Ashforth
Project designer: Danielle Maccarone
Permissions researchers: Lumina Datamatics
Production controller: Renee Tome

Acknowledgements
We would like to thank the following for permission to reproduce copyright material:

Front cover: iStock.com/pixdeluxe; p. 4: UPI/Alamy Stock Photo; p. 5: FPG/Archive Photos/Getty Images; p. 6: Antiqua Print Gallery/Alamy Stock Photo; p. 7: (top) Chroma Collection/Alamy Stock Photo; (bottom) UPI/Alamy Stock Photo; p. 8: dpa picture alliance/Alamy Stock Photo; p. 9: DIMITAR DILKOFF/AFP/Getty Images; p. 10: Patrick Smith/Getty Images Sport/Getty Images; p. 11: Smith Archive/Alamy Stock Photo; p. 12: RBM Vintage Images/Alamy Stock Photo; p. 13: ullstein bild Dtl./ullstein bild/Getty Images; p. 14: (left) Jed Jacobsohn/Getty Images Sport/Getty Images; (right) UPI/Alamy Stock Photo; p. 15: Dean Mouhtaropoulos/Getty Images Sport/Getty Images; p. 16: (top) Avpics/Alamy Stock Photo; (bottom) Isabel Infantes/Alamy Stock Photo; p. 17: ullstein bild Dtl. /ullstein bild/Getty Images; p. 18: Split Seconds/Alamy Stock Photo; p. 19: Popperfoto/Popperfoto/Getty Images; p. 20: Alexander Hassenstein/Bongarts/Getty Images; p. 21: (left) Carl Court/Getty Images Sport/Getty Images; (right) PA Images/Alamy Stock Photo; Title cover; p. 22: noriox/Shutterstock.com; p. 23: ANTONIO SCORZA/AFP/Getty Images; p. 24: Bob Thomas/Bob Thomas Sports Photography/Getty Images; p. 25: Manny Millan/Sports Illustrated/Getty Images; p. 26: MediaPunch Inc/Alamy Stock Photo; p. 27: dpa picture alliance/Alamy Stock Photo; p. 28: United World Wrestling/Getty Images Sport/Getty Images; p. 29: Bettmann/Getty Images; p. 30: PA Images Archive/PA Images/Getty Images; torch background images: Helen/Adobe Stock Photos.

Every effort has been made to trace and acknowledge copyright. However, if any infringement has occurred, the publishers tender their apologies and invite the copyright holders to contact them.

NovaStar

ISBN 978 0 17 033523 2

Cengage Learning Australia
Level 5, 80 Dorcas Street
Southbank VIC 3006 Australia
Phone: 1300 790 853
Email: aust.nelsonprimary@cengage.com

For learning solutions, visit **cengage.com.au**

Printed in China by 1010 Printing International Ltd
1 2 3 4 5 6 7 29 28 27 26 25

Nelson acknowledges the Traditional Owners and Custodians of the lands of all First Nations Peoples. We pay respect to Elders past and present, and extend that respect to all First Nations Peoples today.

Contents

The Spirit of the Olympic Games

The Olympic Games are an international sporting competition. There are the Summer Olympic Games, the Winter Olympic Games and the Paralympic Games. Sportspeople from around the world compete in all sorts of events, using all parts of their bodies, in many different environments.

The official Olympic Games **motto** is "Citius, Altius, Fortius – Communiter", which is **Latin** for "Faster, Higher, Stronger – Together". Most of this motto is about the physical aspects of the Olympic Games – how fast you run, swim, ski or wheel; how high you jump or throw; and how strong you are to lift heavy weights or wrestle someone to the ground.

Athletes from around the world participate in the closing ceremony of the 2012 Summer Olympic Games in London, UK.

But the last word of the motto, "Together", represents the spirit of the Olympic Games. The spirit is in the way the sportspeople compete. It's about being a good sport, winning against all odds and the belief that competing is more important than winning.

Many Olympic athletes have competed with the Olympic spirit. Some athletes won gold medals, but many didn't. This book contains the stories of some of these spirited Olympians.

Together at the Closing Ceremony

Every Olympic Games has an opening and a closing ceremony. At the opening ceremony, athletes enter the stadium one country at a time. But at the closing ceremony, they enter the stadium all together. The idea for all athletes to gather as a united group at the closing ceremony came from an Australian schoolboy for the Melbourne Olympic Games in 1956. It represents the Olympic spirit.

Athletes gather as a united group in the closing ceremony of the 1956 Summer Olympic Games in Melbourne, Australia.

An Overview of the Olympic Games

The Ancient Olympic Games

The Olympic Games were first held in ancient Greece in 776 **BCE** in Olympia. These games were more of a religious festival than a sporting one. Historians believe that at the first games, there was only one sporting event: a running race of about 200 metres. The last ancient Olympic Games were held in 393 **CE**.

Olympia, Ancient Greece

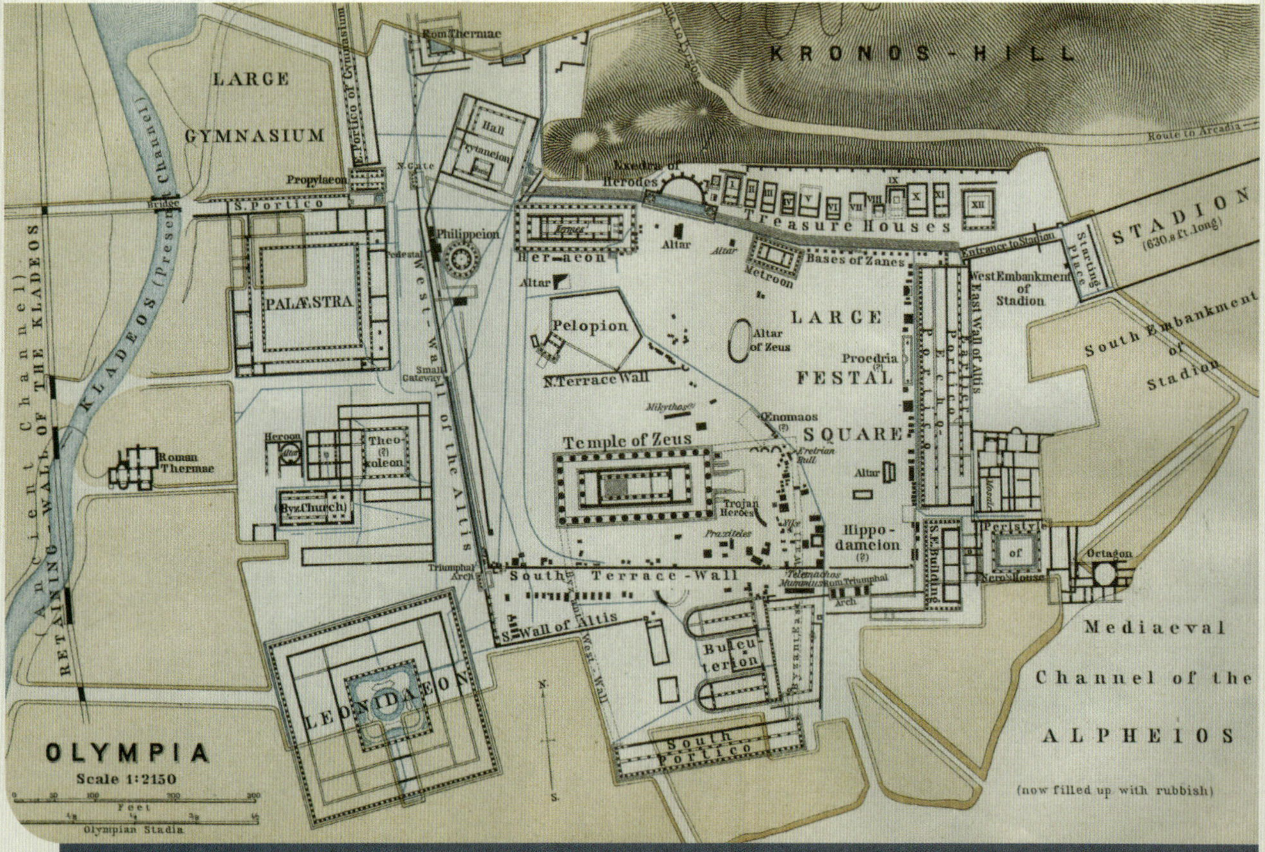

This map shows where the first Olympic Games were held in Olympia, Ancient Greece.

The Modern Olympic Games

The modern Olympic Games were first held in Athens, Greece, in 1896. The **founder** of the modern Olympic Games was a Frenchman, Pierre de Coubertin. Pierre had the skills and passion to organise a return of the games. He also had connections to many influential people who helped him.

Since then, the Olympic Games have been held every four years, although there have been a few exceptions. They did not go ahead in 1916 because of World War I and in 1940 and 1944 because of World War II. The 2020 Olympic Games were held in 2021 because of the global Covid-19 pandemic.

At the Summer Olympic Games, athletes run, swim, cycle, lift, shoot arrows, wrestle, twist their bodies through the air in gymnastics, and much more.

Pierre de Coubertin

Pierre de Coubertin worked to encourage students to attend and complete high school in France. One of his main areas of interest was school sport, and his wish to restart the Olympic Games was connected to that interest.

American gymnast Simone Biles competes in the women's balance beam final at the 2024 Summer Olympic Games in Paris, France.

The Winter Olympic Games

The Winter Olympic Games were first held in Chamonix, France, in 1924. Until 1992, they took place in the same year as the Summer Olympic Games. Since 1994, they have occurred in the even-numbered years when the summer games are not held.

The Winter Olympic Games can only be held in cold climates where there is natural snow and ice. Some **artificial** snow and ice is also used.

At the Winter Olympic Games, athletes ski, skate, fly through the air and slide head-first down steep slopes in freezing conditions.

German athlete Alexander Gassner competes in the men's skeleton event at the 2022 Winter Olympics Games in Beijing, China.

The Paralympic Games

The Paralympic Games are for athletes with disabilities. The first official Paralympic Games were held in Rome, Italy, in 1960 and featured 400 athletes from 23 countries. Since 1988, they have been held alongside the Summer Olympic Games, and alongside the Winter Olympic Games since 1992.

At the Paralympic Games, athletes swim, cycle, ski, skate, lift, and kick, hit and throw balls.

Athletes compete in the 100m T63 athletic event at the 2024 Paralympic Games in Paris, France.

Being a Good Sport

What is a "Good Sport"?

Being a good sport is the quality of playing sport in the right manner. This includes respecting the opposition, sticking to the rules of the game and accepting defeat graciously.

Athletes have shown how to be a good sport in many different ways at the Olympic Games.

Gianmarco Tamberi of Italy and Mutaz Essa Barshim of Qatar decided to share the gold medal in high jump at the 2020 Summer Olympic Games in Tokyo after Barshim was injured in the final.

At the 1964 Winter Olympic Games in Innsbruck, Austria, Italian **bobsled** competitor Eugenio Monti showed what being a good sport is. He and his bobsled partner had recorded the fastest time in their event and were on track to win the gold medal. There was only one team left to compete: the British team.

However, a bolt from the British team's sled broke before they had their turn. Monti unscrewed a bolt from his sled and lent it to the British pair, who beat the Italians' time and won the gold medal. Without the bolt, the British team's sled would not have stayed together.

Monti commented afterwards, saying Nash (one of the British sledders) "didn't win because I gave him the bolt. He won because he had the fastest run".

The Pierre de Coubertin World Fair Play Trophy

Sportspeople who demonstrate being a good sport can be awarded the Pierre de Coubertin World Fair Play Trophy. This trophy is presented by the International Fair Play Committee when someone displays an exceptional act of fair play. It is open to all sportspeople, not just Olympians. The first trophy ever awarded was to Eugenio Monti in 1964.

Eugenio Monti congratulates Tony Nash at the 1964 Winter Olympic Games.

Luz Long and Jesse Owens

The 1936 Summer Olympic Games in Berlin, Germany, were **controversial**. The leader of Germany at the time, Adolf Hitler, wanted to show the world how powerful his country was becoming. He believed that white people were **superior** to people of colour.

At the time, the best long jumper in the world was the African-American jumper, Jesse Owens. He was expected to easily win the long jump event. He had already won gold medals in running events, although Hitler had refused to congratulate him. Hitler was in the stadium for the long jump and was hoping that Luz Long, the German jumper, would win.

Adolf Hitler watches from the crowd at the 1936 Summer Olympic Games in Berlin, Germany.

Things went wrong for Owens early on. He did a **foul** jump when practising, but the German official told Owens that it would count as one of his jumps. The official was letting Long take as many practice jumps as he liked.

If long jumpers do three foul jumps in a row, they are out of the competition. Owens's second jump was also a foul, which meant that he would be out of the competition if his third jump was a foul, too. Long approached Owens and, much to Hitler's fury, gave Owens some advice about where to take off from with his next jump.

Owens did as Long had suggested, and he won the gold medal with the longest jump. Long finished second. The two athletes then paraded in front of Hitler with their arms around each other.

Jesse Owens and Luz Long competed against each other in the long jump event.

Bjørnar Håkensmoen and Sara Renner

At the Winter Olympic Games in Turin, Italy, in 2006, the Canadian **cross-country** skiing team looked set to win gold in the women's team sprint event. Then, one of their skiers, Sara Renner, broke a ski pole during the race and the Canadians slipped from first to fourth place. A Norwegian team official, Bjørnar Håkensmoen, grabbed a spare pole near him and handed it to Renner.

The Canadian team then worked its way up to second place and won the silver medal. Norway finished fourth. Håkensmoen's actions cost his team the bronze medal, but Håkensmoen later said, "If you win but don't help somebody when you should have, what win is that?"

Norwegian team official Bjørnar Håkensmoen (left) showed the Olympic spirit to Sara Renner and Beckie Scott (right) from Canada in the cross-country skiing event at the 2006 Turin Winter Olympic Games.

Stuart Jones and Toni Mould

At the Tokyo Paralympic Games in 2021, the men's and women's **paracycling** events were held at the same time. Australian Paralympic cyclist Stuart Jones was competing in the men's event when he noticed that the South African Paralympic cyclist Toni Mould was struggling to get up a hill in the women's event. Jones abandoned his race and went back to ride beside Mould, encouraging her up the hill. Even though Mould was in last place, Jones rode next to her until she passed the finish line.

Afterwards, Jones said, "On my last lap as I hit the bottom of the climb I came across Toni Mould ... here's Toni, a true champion going up the climb and I thought, well, if I can help her up the hill then my day here has been worthwhile."

Stuart Jones demonstrated the Olympic spirit at the Paralympic Games in Tokyo, Japan, in 2021.

Against All Odds

Hurdles Athletes Face

The Olympic Games are supposed to determine who the fastest and strongest athletes are in the world. But just getting to the Olympic Games is an achievement.

Most athletes who perform well at the Olympics come from countries that are wealthy or have governments that support their sportspeople. But many athletes come from countries that are unable or unwilling to provide the same support.

Some athletes suffer painful injuries while competing at the Olympic Games.

The Refugee Olympic Team athletes wave to spectators during the opening ceremony of the 2024 Summer Olympic Games in Paris, France.

Some governments do not allow women to compete in sport. Women from these countries may have to live somewhere else to train and compete to make it to the Olympic Games.

Some countries may be at war when the Olympic Games take place, which makes it hard for athletes to leave to compete at the games and then return to their countries.

Once at the Olympic Games, some athletes suffer injuries and other **setbacks** that they did not imagine would happen to them.

Overcoming these hurdles shows that the Olympic Games are about far more than being the best athlete. They are about determination, courage and **inner strength**.

Shoeless

Shoes are essential for runners, but the best shoes often cost a lot of money. Ethiopian athlete Abebe Bikila won the marathon at the 1960 Summer Olympic Games in Rome in bare feet, after his shoes fell apart a few days before the race. He could not find or afford another suitable pair.

Abebe Bikila competes in the marathon without shoes at the 1960 Summer Olympic Games in Rome, Italy.

Bill Roycroft

At the 1960 Summer Olympic Games in Rome, Italy, Bill Roycroft was one of Australia's four riders in the three-day **equestrian** competition. The competition consisted of three events: dressage, cross-country and show jumping. During the cross-country event, Roycroft fell from his horse and was knocked unconscious. He was flown to hospital, where doctors found he had a broken shoulder, bruised ribs, a dislocated collarbone and a brain injury.

Lying in hospital, Roycroft found out that one of his teammates' horses had also been injured. This meant that his teammate could not ride in the final showjumping event, as riders were not allowed to ride anyone else's horse. The Australians were winning the competition but needed three teammates to complete the final event or they would be disqualified.

Bill Roycroft competes in the equestrian competition at the 1960 Summer Olympic Games in Rome, Italy.

Roycroft demanded to be released from the hospital, but the doctors refused. They even hid his clothes. Eventually, the doctors let Roycroft go when he threatened to walk out in his underwear.

Because of Roycroft's injuries, his teammates had to dress him in his riding gear, lift him into his horse's saddle and place the reins in his good hand. Despite all this, Roycroft and his horse cleared all 12 jumps and secured Australia's gold medal. It was one of the most courageous achievements in Olympic history.

Bill Roycroft's actions helped his teammates win gold at the Summer Olympic Games in 1960. Robert Lawrence Morgan (centre) and Neale Lavis (left) also won individual gold and silver medals.

Petra Majdic

At the 2010 Winter Olympic Games in Vancouver, Canada, Petra Majdic from Slovenia competed in the cross-country skiing sprint event. While practising, she slid off the track, fell 3 metres and broke several ribs. She managed to compete in the first round of the event but then collapsed and was taken to hospital.

Majdic came back to compete in the quarter-final, then the semi-final, where one of her ribs **punctured** her lung. In agony, she still competed in the final and won the bronze medal.

Instead of going straight back to hospital, she attended the medal ceremony in a wheelchair.

Petra Majdic celebrates her bronze medal at the 2010 Winter Olympic Games in Vancouver, Canada, after competing with injuries.

Zakia Khudadadi and Hossain Rasouli

Just before the Paralympic Games in Tokyo, Japan, in 2021, a group called the Taliban took over the country of Afghanistan. The country was in chaos, with thousands of people at the airport trying to flee from the Taliban. This was partly because when the group had last been in power, years earlier, they **persecuted** many people, particularly girls and women.

Zakia Khudadadi and Hossain Rasouli had been chosen to represent Afghanistan in Tokyo, but they could not get out of their country. Khudadadi was also a woman, so the Taliban would probably not allow her to compete.

With help from international organisations, a secret flight was organised from Kabul to Paris, then to Tokyo.

Khudadadi competed in **taekwondo** and Rasouli in the long jump. For them, winning a medal was not as important as having gone to the Olympic Games in the first place.

Zakia Khudadadi (left) and Hossain Rasouli (right) of Afghanistan compete at the Paralympic Games in Tokyo, Japan, in 2021.

Winning Isn't Everything

The Olympic Creed

The Olympic **creed** reads:
"The important thing in life is not the triumph, but the fight; the essential thing is not to have won, but to have fought well."

It was written after Pierre de Coubertin heard an American **bishop**, Ethelbert Talbot, give a speech at St Paul's Cathedral in London during the 1908 Olympic Games.

In his speech, Talbot said, "The Games themselves are better than the race and the prize" and "though only one may wear the **laurel wreath**, all may share the equal joy of the contest".

These words inspired the writing of the Olympic creed, which in turn inspired many sportspeople.

The Olympic Symbol

The Olympic movement has a symbol: five interlinked rings of blue, black, red, yellow and green. They represent the five inhabited continents on Earth (counting North and South America as one continent), and the coming together of athletes from those continents.

Eric Moussambani

Eric Moussambani represented the African country of Equatorial Guinea in swimming at the 2000 Summer Olympic Games in Sydney, Australia. His path to the Olympic Games had not been easy.

Olympic swimming pools are 50 metres long, but Moussambani had to train in a 12-metre pool because there were no 50-metre pools in his country. There was neither the money nor the demand to build such large pools in Equatorial Guinea. The first time Moussambani swam in a 50-metre pool was in his **heat** of the 100-metre freestyle race in Sydney.

Moussambani's time was the slowest in Olympic history. At one point, **officials** became worried he would need to be rescued from the water. However, the crowd cheered him on and he did not give up. He finished the race, swimming a personal-best time. As the creed says, "the essential thing is not to have won, but to have fought well", and Moussambani fought well.

Eric Moussambani dives into his men's 100-metre freestyle heat at the 2000 Summer Olympic Games in Sydney, Australia.

Jamaican Bobsled Team

Jamaica is a country in the Caribbean, where the climate is warm all year round. There is no snow in Jamaica, so the world was stunned when Jamaica entered a team into the four-man bobsled event at the 1988 Winter Olympic Games in Calgary, Canada.

The idea for a Jamaican bobsled team came from two Americans, George Fitch and William Maloney, who were living in Jamaica. They wanted to march at an Olympic Games opening ceremony, so they needed to get some sort of team together. They saw kart racing on TV in Jamaica, and thought it was close enough to bobsledding. Fitch and Maloney went to the Jamaican army to find fit, healthy men and also held trials in wooden karts. Finally, they chose their team. They practised with a kart on firm ground in Jamaica, and later in an ice-hockey rink in the USA.

The Jamaican men's bobsled team competes at the 1988 Winter Olympic Games in Calgary, Canada.

The team arrived at the Olympic Games without a proper four-man bobsled and had to borrow a spare bobsled from the Canadian team. It was the first time they had ever seen an ice-covered bobsled run.

The team crashed racing down the track and officially finished in 30th place. The crowd loved them because they were such unlikely competitors. Their story became so popular that, in 1993, the film *Cool Runnings* was made about the team. The Jamaicans had little chance of winning a medal against their experienced opposition, but just getting to the games was a triumph.

Spectators cheer on the Jamaican Olympic bobsled team.

Ryan Boyle

Ryan Boyle competed in paracycling for the United States at the 2016 Paralympics in Rio de Janeiro, Brazil.

When he was ten, Boyle was hit by a truck while riding his bike. He was airlifted to hospital and had emergency surgery on his brain. Doctors did not expect him to survive. He spent two months in a **coma**, and when he woke up, the only movement he could make was to wiggle one finger.

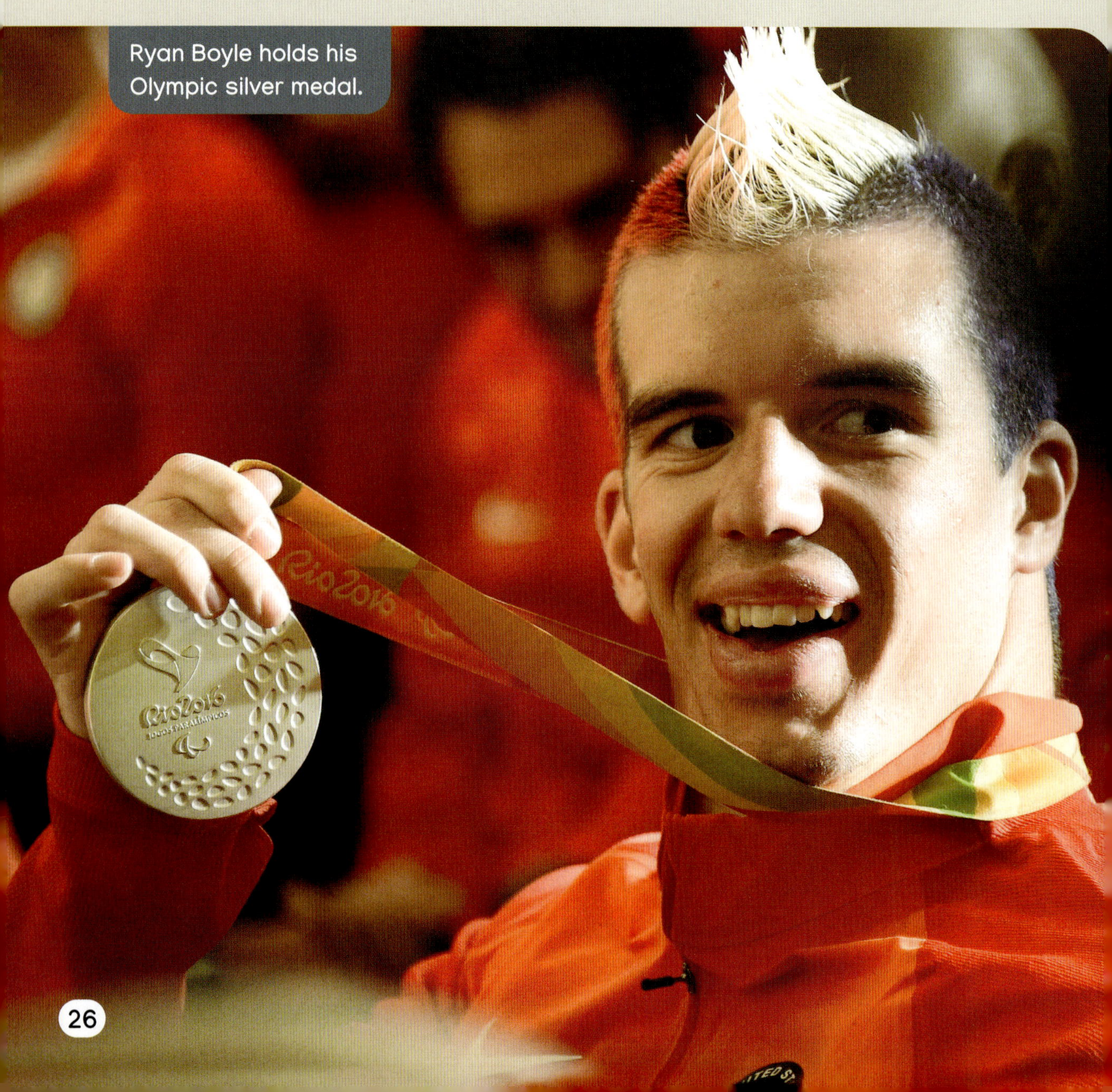

Ryan Boyle holds his Olympic silver medal.

Slowly, he relearnt how to breathe, swallow, talk, eat, stand, sit and take steps. Even then, he used a wheelchair most of the time.

Despite the accident, which he didn't remember, Boyle learnt how to ride a bicycle again and trained hard to make the American team for the 2016 Paralympics. He won a silver medal in the men's T1-2 time trial event.

Ryan Boyle (left) celebrates with Hans-Peter Durst (centre) and David Stone (right) on the podium after winning silver in the men's T1–2 time trial event.

Competing in the Right Spirit

Media coverage of the Olympic Games, whether on TV or online, usually focuses on the winners and the table that shows which countries are winning the most medals.

But behind those winners are stories, courage and spirit that are just as important, if not more so, as the medals.

There are athletes from small nations who face all kinds of challenges just to make it to the Olympics. Even if they finish a race behind all the other competitors, they have still succeeded.

There are examples of being a good sport, such as when a competitor stops racing to help someone who has fallen or is struggling.

And while winning might be the goal, competing in the right spirit is far more important.

Being a good sport and competing with the Olympic spirit is just as important as winning a medal.

Eddie *the* Eagle

Ski News Daily | 23 February 1988 | Calgary, Canada

Today, at the Winter Olympic Games, we witnessed the most unlikely ski jumper of all time compete in his second, and final, event. Michael Edwards, known as Eddie the Eagle, finished last in the large hill individual ski event, jumping 71 metres. The winner jumped 118 metres. Edwards also finished last nine days ago in the normal hill individual event, but his unlikely appearance in the ski-jumping events has made him a crowd favourite.

Eddie the Eagle soars over the crowd.

Edwards is the first person from Britain to compete in the ski jump at the Olympic Games. He decided to take up ski jumping after a ski trip, not because he was good at it, but because there were no other people in Britain doing it. It was easier for him to qualify for the Olympic Games in that sport.

There are no ski-jump training courses in Britain, so Edwards learnt the basic techniques on dirt slopes, then practised on ski slopes in the United States. He had to pay for everything himself while he was learning because Britain did not have a sporting organisation in charge of ski jumping from which he could receive funding.

After his final jump at the Winter Olympics, Edwards said, "I had no money, no training facilities, no snow, no ski jumps, no trainer, but I still managed to ski jump for my country, and getting there was my gold."

Edwards might not have soared like an eagle – in fact, he said, "I was probably closer to the ostrich" – but he reached heights no one expected.

Eddie the Eagle celebrates after a successful jump.

Glossary

artificial (*adjective*)	made by humans, rather than occurring naturally
BCE (*noun*)	before the common era
bishop (*noun*)	a senior figure in the Christian religion
bobsled (*noun*)	a small vehicle that is ridden down a steep, icy slope at high speeds
CE (*noun*)	the common era
coma (*noun*)	a state of being unconscious
controversial (*adjective*)	causing disagreement
creed (*noun*)	beliefs or aims which guide someone's actions
cross-country (*adjective*)	racing across open land
equestrian (*adjective*)	to do with horse riding
foul (*noun*)	a move that is not legal or allowed
founder (*noun*)	someone who sets up an organisation
heat (*noun*)	an early race that determines who races in the finals
inner strength (*noun*)	mental strength
Latin (*noun*)	a language common in ancient Rome
laurel wreath (*noun*)	a round headpiece made from twigs and leaves from the bay laurel plant
motto (*noun*)	a short sentence that expresses certain beliefs
officials (*noun*)	people in charge
paracycling (*noun*)	the sport of cycling for people with disabilities
persecuted (*verb*)	treated people badly because of their beliefs or cultural background
punctured (*verb*)	pierced or stabbed
setbacks (*noun*)	things that go wrong
superior (*adjective*)	higher in rank or quality
taekwondo (*noun*)	a Korean martial art similar to karate
time trial (*noun*)	a cycling event where riders try to ride the fastest time, rather than racing against each other

Index